Francis Frith's
South Wales

Photographic Memories

Francis Frith's
South Wales

Tony Cornish and James Plant

FRITH
BOOK Co

First published in the United Kingdom in 2002 by
Frith Book Company Ltd

Hardback Edition 2002
ISBN 1-85937-519-7

British Library Cataloguing in Publication Data

Francis Frith's South Wales
Tony Cornish and James Plant

Frith Book Company Ltd
Frith's Barn, Teffont,
Salisbury, Wiltshire SP3 5QP
Tel: +44 (0) 1722 716 376
Email: info@francisfrith.co.uk
www.francisfrith.co.uk

Printed and bound in Great Britain

Front Cover: Newport, Commercial Street c1955 N25141

AS WITH ANY HISTORICAL DATABASE THE FRITH ARCHIVE IS CONSTANTLY BEING CORRECTED AND IMPROVED
AND THE PUBLISHERS WOULD WELCOME INFORMATION ON OMISSIONS OR INACCURACIES

Contents

Francis Frith: *Victorian Pioneer*

FRANCIS FRITH, Victorian founder of the world-famous photographic archive, was a complex and multi-talented man. A devout Quaker and a highly successful Victorian businessman, he was both philosophic by nature and pioneering in outlook.

By 1855 Francis Frith had already established a wholesale grocery business in Liverpool, and sold it for the astonishing sum of £200,000, which is the equivalent today of over £15,000,000. Now a multi-millionaire, he was able to indulge his passion for travel. As a child he had pored over travel books written by early explorers, and his fancy and imagination had been stirred by family holidays to the sublime mountain regions of Wales and Scotland. 'What a land of spirit-stirring and enriching scenes and places!' he had written. He was to return to these scenes of grandeur in later years to 'recapture the thousands of vivid and tender memories', but with a different purpose. Now in his thirties, and captivated by the new science of photography, Frith set out on a series of pioneering journeys to the Nile regions that occupied him from 1856 until 1860.

Intrigue and Adventure

He took with him on his travels a specially-designed wicker carriage that acted as both dark-room and sleeping chamber. These far-flung journeys were packed with intrigue and adventure. In his life story, written when he was sixty-three, Frith tells of being held captive by bandits, and of fighting 'an awful midnight battle to the very point of surrender with a deadly pack of hungry, wild dogs'. Sporting flowing Arab costume, Frith arrived at Akaba by camel seventy years before Lawrence, where he encountered 'desert princes and rival sheikhs, blazing with jewel-hilted swords'.

During these extraordinary adventures he was assiduously exploring the desert regions bordering the Nile and patiently recording the antiquities and peoples with his camera. He was the first photographer to venture beyond the sixth cataract. Africa was still the mysterious 'Dark Continent', and Stanley and Livingstone's historic meeting was a decade into the future. The conditions for picture taking confound belief. He laboured for hours in his wicker dark-room in the sweltering heat of the desert, while the volatile chemicals fizzed dangerously in their trays. Often he was forced to work in remote tombs and caves where conditions were cooler. Back in London he exhibited his photographs and was 'rapturously cheered' by members of the Royal Society. His reputation as a photographer was made overnight. An eminent modern historian has likened their impact on the population of the time to that on our own generation of the first photographs taken on the surface of the moon.

Venture of a Life-Time

Characteristically, Frith quickly spotted the opportunity to create a new business as a specialist publisher of photographs. He lived in an era of immense and sometimes violent change. For the poor in the early part of Victoria's reign work was a drudge and the hours long, and people had precious little free time to enjoy themselves. Most had no transport other than a cart or gig at their disposal, and had not travelled far beyond the boundaries of their own town or village. However,

by the 1870s, the railways had threaded their way across the country, and Bank Holidays and half-day Saturdays had been made obligatory by Act of Parliament. All of a sudden the ordinary working man and his family were able to enjoy days out and see a little more of the world.

With characteristic business acumen, Francis Frith foresaw that these new tourists would enjoy having souvenirs to commemorate their days out. In 1860 he married Mary Ann Rosling and set out with the intention of photographing every city, town and village in Britain. For the next thirty years he travelled the country by train and by pony and trap, producing fine photographs of seaside resorts and beauty spots that were keenly bought by millions of Victorians. These prints were painstakingly pasted into family albums and pored over during the dark nights of winter, rekindling precious memories of summer excursions.

The Rise of Frith & Co

Frith's studio was soon supplying retail shops all over the country. To meet the demand he gathered about him a small team of photographers, and published the work of independent artist-photographers of the calibre of Roger Fenton and Francis Bedford. In order to gain some understanding of the scale of Frith's business one only has to look at the catalogue issued by Frith & Co in 1886: it runs to some 670 pages, listing not only many thousands of views of the British Isles but also many photographs of most European countries, and China, Japan, the USA and Canada – note the sample page shown above from the hand-written *Frith & Co* ledgers detailing pictures taken. By 1890 Frith had created the greatest specialist photographic publishing company in the world,

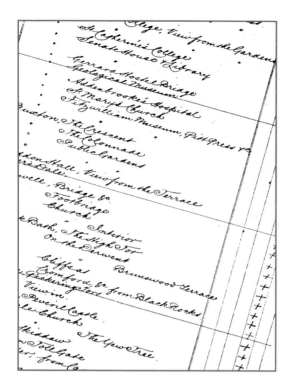

Frith's death, a new card measuring 5.5 x 3.5 inches became the standard format, but it was not until 1902 that the divided back came into being, with address and message on one face and a full-size illustration on the other. *Frith & Co* were in the vanguard of postcard development, and Frith's sons Eustace and Cyril continued their father's monumental task, expanding the number of views offered to the public and recording more and more places in Britain, as the coasts and countryside were opened up to mass travel.

Francis Frith died in 1898 at his villa in Cannes, his great project still growing. The archive he created continued in business for another seventy years. By 1970 it contained over a third of a million pictures of 7,000 cities, towns and villages. The massive photographic record Frith has left to us stands as a living monument to a special and very remarkable man.

with over 2,000 outlets – more than the combined number that Boots and WH Smith have today! The picture on the right shows the *Frith & Co* display board at Ingleton in the Yorkshire Dales. Beautifully constructed with mahogany frame and gilt inserts, it could display up to a dozen local scenes.

Postcard Bonanza

The ever-popular holiday postcard we know today took many years to develop. In 1870 the Post Office issued the first plain cards, with a pre-printed stamp on one face. In 1894 they allowed other publishers' cards to be sent through the mail with an attached adhesive halfpenny stamp. Demand grew rapidly, and in 1895 a new size of postcard was permitted called the court card, but there was little room for illustration. In 1899, a year after

Frith's Archive: *A Unique Legacy*

FRANCIS FRITH'S legacy to us today is of immense significance and value, for the magnificent archive of evocative photographs he created provides a unique record of change in 7,000 cities, towns and villages throughout Britain over a century and more. Frith and his fellow studio photographers revisited locations many times down the years to update their views, compiling for us an enthralling and colourful pageant of British life and character.

We tend to think of Frith's sepia views of Britain as nostalgic, for most of us use them to conjure up memories of places in our own lives with which we have family associations. It often makes us forget that to Francis Frith they were records of daily life as it was actually being lived in the cities, towns and villages of his day. The Victorian age was one of great and often bewildering change for ordinary people, and though the pictures evoke an

impression of slower times, life was as busy and hectic as it is today.

We are fortunate that Frith was a photographer of the people, dedicated to recording the minutiae of everyday life. For it is this sheer wealth of visual data, the painstaking chronicle of changes in dress, transport, street layouts, buildings, housing, engineering and landscape that captivates us so much today. His remarkable images offer us a powerful link with the past and with the lives of our ancestors.

Today's Technology

Computers have now made it possible for Frith's many thousands of images to be accessed almost instantly. In the Frith archive today, each photograph is carefully 'digitised' then stored on a CD Rom. Frith archivists can locate a single photograph amongst thousands within seconds. Views can be catalogued and sorted under a variety of categories of place and content to the immediate benefit of researchers.

Inexpensive reference prints can be created for them at the touch of a mouse button, and a wide range of books and other printed materials assembled and published for a wider, more general readership - in the next twelve months over a hundred Frith local history titles will be published! The day-to-day workings of the archive are very different from how they were in Francis Frith's time: imagine the herculean task of sorting through eleven tons of glass negatives as Frith had to do to locate a particular sequence of pictures! Yet

THE FRANCIS FRITH COLLECTION

Photographic publishers since 1860

HOME | PHOTO SEARCH | BOOKS | PORTFOLIO | GALLERY   MY CART
Products | History | Other Collections | Contact us | Help?

your town,
your village

365,000 photographs of 7,000 towns and villages, taken between 1860 & 1970.

The Frith Archive
The Frith Archive is the remarkable legacy of its energetic and visionary founder. Today, the Frith archive is the only nationally important archive of its kind still in private ownership.

The Collection is world-renowned for the extraordinary quality of its images.

The Gallery
This month The Frith Gallery features images from "Frith's Egypt".

News...
Image update complete.
An additional 5,000 images have been added and the quality of all images has now been improved.

Sample Chapters available.
The first selection of sample chapters from the Frith Book Co.'s extensive range is now available. All are offered in Pdf format for easy downloading and viewing.

explore
FRITH
Search thousands of photographs from one of the worlds' great archives.

Town search

County search
Select a county

the FRITHgallery

See Frith at www.francisfrith.co.uk

the archive still prides itself on maintaining the same high standards of excellence laid down by Francis Frith, including the painstaking cataloguing and indexing of every view.

It is curious to reflect on how the internet now allows researchers in America and elsewhere greater instant access to the archive than Frith himself ever enjoyed. Many thousands of individual views can be called up on screen within seconds on one of the Frith internet sites, enabling people living continents away to revisit the streets of their ancestral home town, or view places in Britain where they have enjoyed holidays. Many overseas researchers welcome the chance to view special theme selections, such as transport, sports, costume and ancient monuments.

We are certain that Francis Frith would have heartily approved of these modern developments in imaging techniques, for he himself was always working at the very limits of Victorian photographic technology.

The Value of the Archive Today

Because of the benefits brought by the computer, Frith's images are increasingly studied by social historians, by researchers into genealogy and ancestory, by architects, town planners, and by teachers and schoolchildren involved in local history projects.

In addition, the archive offers every one of us an opportunity to examine the places where we and our families have lived and worked down the years. Highly successful in Frith's own era, the archive is now, a century and more on, entering a new phase of popularity.

The Past in Tune with the Future

Historians consider the Francis Frith Collection to be of prime national importance. It is the only archive of its kind remaining in private ownership and has been valued at a million pounds. However, this figure is now rapidly increasing as digital technology enables more and more people around the world to enjoy its benefits.

Francis Frith's archive is now housed in an historic timber barn in the beautiful village of Teffont in Wiltshire. Its founder would not recognize the archive office as it is today. In place of the many thousands of dusty boxes containing glass plate negatives and an all-pervading odour of photographic chemicals, there are now ranks of computer screens. He would be amazed to watch his images travelling round the world at unimaginable speeds through network and internet lines.

The archive's future is both bright and exciting. Francis Frith, with his unshakeable belief in making photographs available to the greatest number of people, would undoubtedly approve of what is being done today with his lifetime's work. His photographs, depicting our shared past, are now bringing pleasure and enlightenment to millions around the world a century and more after his death.

South Wales - *An Introduction*

WHEN WE THINK of South Wales, the first things that may come to mind are coal and iron. However, there is so much more to this beautiful area of the country. Before the coal and ironworks took hold in the area, the main industry was the land itself. Today, the rolling fields bear witness to this most ancient form of employment. It was principally during the 19th century that the extractive industries took hold, which meant a meteoric rise in population in Merthyr Tydfil, Cardiff, Newport and many other places. The towns sprang up where before there were none, bearing witness to the rich seams beneath the green valleys. Entrepreneurs such as the Guests and the Crawshays, the owners of Dowlais and Cyfartha, made vast sums of money, and this was reflected in their architectural legacies. Richard Crawshay was so successful that at his death he had become one of Britain's first millionaires. As for the coal industry, it was said that

in the 19th century South Wales coal ran the British Navy. South Wales's industrial importance has recently been recognised by the designation of Blaenafon Big Pit as a World Heritage Site.

Throughout the area there are numerous castles, some of which were built on Roman or earlier sites; some are of Norman origin, and some are pure Welsh, and this tells of the sometimes volatile politics of South Wales in earlier times. More recently, it has been changes in the county boundaries that have rung the territorial changes. The most recent change is that Newport has been made a city.

This book is a short excursion around what is without doubt one of the country's most fascinating areas and one that is rich in history. We do hope that you enjoy the memories that lie within these pages.

Abercynon, General View c1965 A191056
The town has an important place in industrial history, for it is the southern end of the railway line on which the first steam locomotive ran in 1804. Richard Trevithick's tramway from Merthyr to Abercynon led the way for the railway boom of the 1840s. This development, of course, meant the demise of the canals.

Aberdare, c1955 A192066
An industrial town situated at the joining of the river Dar and river Cynon. At the beginning of the 19th Century Aberdare was a village within an agricultural district. The population increased during the first half of the century with the discovery of an abundant supply of coal and iron ore.

◄ **Aberfan**
Aberfan Road c1965
A193009
This valley community became the focus of a nation's grief when in 1966 Pontglas School and a row of adjacent houses were buried under a sliding coal tip. Of the 144 who died in the tragedy, 116 were children. The site is now a memorial garden.

◄ **Abergavenny, The Castle 1914** 67673
Abergavenny's origins lie in the Roman fort of Gobannium, established by the Romans to protect their road up the river Usk. Hameline de Balun established the first castle here between 1085 and 1138, and it later came into the ownership of William de Braose. It was in this castle in 1176 that William had his revenge on his Welsh enemies for the killing of his uncle. He invited them all as guests to his castle at Christmas of that year as a gesture of reconciliation - then had them all murdered!

▼ **Abertillery
Penybont and Cwmtill
c1955** A279022
Here we have a panoramic view of this industrial town. Note the extensive terraced housing typical of communities like this, which developed in the 19th century as industrial towns.

◄ **Abertillery
Somerset Street c1955** A279042
We are in the town centre. Note the branch of Woolworth's just visible at the end of the street, and the branch of Dewhurst the butchers among the other shops on the right.

Bargoed
High Street 1951 B300022
Bargoed was once a village; it is situated in a long valley.
The population grew in the 19th century, especially after the
opening of the colliery here in 1897. Today the town is most
notable for its rows of terraces winding round the valley contours.
This photograph captures some of the ornate town centre
architecture. Note the sign for the National Assistance Board Area
Office (bottom right), set up to assist those who slipped through
the net following the establishment of National Insurance
contributions in the 1940s.

Barry, Thompson Street 1925 77490
The docks at Barry were established between 1884 and 1899 by David Davies, a coal exporter who objected to paying levies to Cardiff. Between 1884 and 1920 the town's population grew from 100 to an estimated 40,000. Note the 1920s style of the lady's and child's dresses.

Barry, Holton Road 1903 50852
There is much to see in this picture, including the flat-capped men looking directly at the photographer on the right, and the more casual observers further up the street. Note the two women deep in conversation on the left, the dog in the middle of the street (this would result in its certain death today) and the handcart on the right. B G Davies, 'Solicitor and Notary', have their offices on the corner, with the Cash Clothing Co and Newman's the chemist further down the road.

**Barry Island
The Sands 1910** 62560
Barry Island was a popular holiday destination for the valley miners for their annual 'miners' fortnight'; suits, caps, full-length skirts and hats appear to be the order of the day. Note the stall towards the centre of the picture.

Boverton, The Post Office 1967 B397052
The post office (on the left of the picture), under the management of F G Fitchett, is apparently the fulcrum of village life. Note the advertisements for groceries and provisions, ice-cream and tobacco products. Note also the vending machines to the left of the door.

Bridgend, The Old Stone Bridge 1898 41200
The Welsh name for Bridgend is 'Yr Hen Bont'. This photograph was taken from the new bridge looking towards the old bridge, which is built of the local Quarella stone and dates from the early 15th century. It was partly destroyed on 21 August 1775 by a large flood - two of the original small arches were replaced by the single large span we can see here, giving it an asymmetrical appearance. The cottage with the bay window at the right-hand end of the bridge is St John's, or Bridge Cottage, dating from 1460; it was once used as a courtroom pending the completion of the new town hall. It was demolished in 1966 amid much local protest.

Bridgend
Coity Castle and the Church 1898 41202
The church is just visible to the left of the picture. Coity Castle is roughly two miles to the
north-west of Bridgend; a somewhat unusual feature is that the castle was not built on the
highest ground on this site - there is higher ground nearby. The earlier parts of the castle date
from the 12th century, but most of the ruins are 14th-century and Tudor. There is a local
legend telling how Payn de Turberville acquired the castle following the Norman conquest of
Glamorgan. The most common way for faithful men to be rewarded for services rendered was
by the giving of lands. William the Conqueror in 1066 promised land to his followers, and this
practice continued as Norman lordlings pressed north and west. Payn was fully expecting to
take possession of Coity when he arrived here; but instead of surrendering the place
immediately, the local chieftain, Morgan, responded by riding out equipped for battle.
However, Morgan took the precaution of riding out in the company of his lovely daughter,
Sybil. Morgan offered Payn a simple choice: fight or marry Sybil and inherit Coity by peaceful
means. Payn chose to marry Sybil, and thereby swore allegiance to Caradoc ap Jestyn. Payn's
descendants were to live at Coity until the end of the 14th century, when the line of de
Turberville died out. The church is noted for two 14th-century de Turberville monuments.

▼ Bridgend, St Illtyd's Church 1898 41204

St Illtyd's is built in the Decorated style and dates from the early 14th century; the nave was rebuilt and a north aisle added in 1849 at a cost of £1,200. The church has a 16th-century crenellated tower with gargoyles and low pinnacles, a clock and a peal of eight bells. The original six bells were recast and two new ones added in 1904 by Richard Knight Pritchard.

▼ Bridgend, Angelton Asylum 1898 41207

This asylum opened in 1864 with 350 patients. By 1875 the population had risen to 557, and there were complaints that it was overcrowded. By 1879 the situation had deteriorated sufficiently for beds to be placed in the corridors, and by 1881 the population had doubled to 661, with about 100 of the patients having to 'board out' - care in the community is nothing new!

▲ Bridgend Ewenny Church 1898

41220
Ewenny Church is in two parts, which are separated by a 13th- to 14th-century rood screen. The nave was the parish church, and the chancel was set aside for the monks.

◀ **Bridgend, The Post Office and Caroline Street 1899** 43350
This photograph was taken from the corner of Caroline Street and Queen Street. Davies's Buildings containing the post office was built in 1892 on the site of the Mackworth Arms (demolished 1890/91). The new cottage hospital, pre-dating this photograph by three years, stands at the top of the street. We can just see the entrance to Caroline Street's first market half way up the street on the right.

Bridgend, Caroline Street 1901 47905 Originally Eastgate Street, this street was renamed Caroline Street after Countess Caroline of Dunraven. She paid for a water pipeline to be laid from a spring near Sarn to a water tap on the corner of Derwen Road and Court Road. Note Olivers shoe shop on the right, and the various advertisements (including Fry's cocoa, left) and Lloyds News (right). Note also the trap coming towards the camera with its two passengers sporting their bonnets.

Bridgend, Ewenny Pottery 1936 87669
Pottery is one of the traditional crafts of the area; this pottery is named after the River Ewenny, which also gives its name to the priory founded in 1141 by Maurice de Londres as a cell of the Gloucester Benedictines. This workshop hails itself as the 'oldest established in Wales'.

Bridgend, Ewenny Pottery 1936 87670
Here are some workmen creating pots in the time-honoured way. Note the pots on the table, all of the same design - was this an early 'production line'?

Bridgend
Dunraven Place c1950 B200002
The memorial behind the railings on the right was
unveiled in November 1921. It was sculpted in
Portland stone by Messrs H H Martyn
& Co Ltd of Cheltenham from a design by Walter
Cook. The figure is of Britannia, with emblems
representing sacrifice and victory below her.
Originally intended to commemorate the soldiers
killed in the First World War, it now also records
the victims of the Second World War, the Women's
British Legion and the Falklands War. Also note the
Provident Clothing and Supply Co Ltd just behind
it, and the decorator on his ladder (centre left).

Bridgend, Dunraven Place 1910 62525
We are looking south-east. The population of Bridgend at this time was approximately 6,000. The Wyndham Hotel is clearly visible on the left, designated as 'of special historical and architectural interest' by the Welsh Office. It was originally four separate premises - a house, a pub, an off-licence and a bookmaker.

Bridgend, Newbridge Fields, the Gorsedd Stones c1955 B2000047
Newbridge Fields were created with a substantial grant from the National Fitness Council. The Gorsedd Stones were erected in preparation for the National Eisteddfod which was to be held here, but the outbreak of World War II delayed this event until 1948.

Caerleon, Christchurch 1899 43655
This church stands in an area with a long-standing Christian heritage: it is recorded that in 314 the Bishop of Caerleon was present at the Synod of Arles, the first general council of western Christianity. The bishopric was later removed to St Davids by Dewi Sant (St David) himself - legend proclaims that this was foretold by Merlin.

Caerleon
The Roman Arch 1931 C4023
The arch is not the genuine article: it is in fact a folly built by one
Miss Elizabeth Morgan in 1820, using stone recovered from the
remains of Roman buildings. The priory which we can see through
the arch was built in about 1179, and is currently a hotel.

Caerphilly
Cardiff Road 1899
43624
Caerphilly is an industrial and market town, perhaps best known for its impressive castle and its eponymous cheese. Caerphilly's name derives from 'caer', meaning a Roman fort, and St Fili.

◄ **Caerphilly**
The Castle c1955 C5122
Here we see the castle after its restoration by the Marquis of Bute. The main residential block, including the great hall, was sited along the south side of the inner curtain wall. The drum towers were also used for accommodation, while the Constable's apartments were situated in the east gatehouse. The wall partly off-picture to the right is a section of the fortified dam.

◄ **Caerphilly, The Castle 1871** 7033

The castle is now much restored by the Marquis of Bute, with its water defences reinstated. The original castle was begun by Gilbert de Clare. His first castle was razed to the ground by the Welsh under Llewelyn in 1268, but he tried again in 1271, only to have this project attacked once again by Llewelyn, who feared the establishment of an English stronghold in this area. Henry III was forced to intervene, and he declared the castle and its surroundings neutral territory. Henry's wishes were to count for little, as de Clare - with the backing of the barons - retook it by force. The building cost was estimated to be somewhere in the region of £5,500-£6,000 - a veritable 13th-century fortune.

▼ **Caerphilly, The Chapel and the Clock Tower 1899** 43627

Caerphlly was primarily an industrial and market town. The cheese of the same name was possibly first made in the market during the 13th or 14th centuries, but the market was closed in the early 1900s (not long after this photograph was taken), and production of the cheese was dispersed to other locations.

◄ **Cardiff, The Castle 1893** 32667

The first Norman castle is thought to have been built in Cardiff in c1081 on the site of a previous Welsh fortification. Extra defensive height was achieved by piling the spoil on top of the circuit walls to create a rampart. In 1106 Robert Curthouse, Duke of Normandy, waged an unsuccessful war with Henry I; the defeated duke was taken to Cardiff Castle. Curthouse's eyes were put out, and he remained a prisoner until his death in 1134.

Cardiff, St Mary Street 1893 32674
Here we can see a range of mid to late Victorian architecture. The road is unsurfaced, but the tramlines are clearly visible - there is a tram in the distance. This is a busy scene, with milk churns on one side of the street and casks of ale on the other (right). Note the various horse-drawn vehicles.

Cardiff, St Mary Street 1896 38709
The statue we can just see on the left is of the Marquis of Bute ; it has since been relocated to make way for traffic improvements. Note the tram just behind the statue, the boys in uniform (centre right) and the various hand- and horse-carts.

Cardiff
The Park Hotel 1893 32679
This fine example of Victorian
architecture was built in 1863, and
brought a flush of style and prestige to
Cardiff. With three hundred rooms in the
heart of the city, it offered a combination
of both opulence and convenience. It is
much the same today, except that it is
now part of the Thistle hotel chain.

Cardiff
The Docks 1893 32696
Shallow-draught paddle steamers were developed specifically for
use in the tidal estuaries, where the water level could become very
low. The steamer in the foreground is the 'Success', a working
boat. Other steamers were also used as pleasure craft.

◄ Cardiff, City Hall 1925
77433
The City Hall was completed in 1904. The dome over the entrance pavilion is topped by an impressive lead dragon. The clock tower is sixty metres high, and is visible from afar. The architect was E A Rickards, a devotee of the baroque style.

◄ Cardiff, Roath Park Lake 1902 49001
Roath Park was laid out in 1894 at a cost of £62,000 - a considerable sum in those days. The land, 132 acres, was presented to the city by Lord Bute. The lake extended to thirty-two acres, and once incorporated a swimming-pool. Skiffs were available for hire, such as the one to the left of the picture. The rower in the foreground would appear to be a park warden, judging by his cap.

Clydach, General View ►
1936 87835
One could be forgiven for assuming that this charming rural scene implies an agricultural history for this area. But that is not entirely true. Clydach is home to an industrial archaeological site, a coke-fired ironworks dating from 1792. It was forced into bankruptcy in 1877.

◄ Clydach
The Lower Fall 1893
32603
Clydach Gorge, once populated by forges, is also well-known for its stands of beech trees which somehow survived the ravages of the charcoal-burners of the time. This woodland scene portrays nothing of the industry in this area - instead it conveys a slightly magical atmosphere.

Clydach
The Wells 1893 32605
It is certainly not unlikely that these men and boys are workers at
what remained of the indigenous ironworking industry after the
1877 collapse. Perhaps they are enjoying a well-earned break from
the rigours of whatever profession they are engaged in.
Note also the lone woman (third from the left) carrying what may
be a 'snap' tin - a meal for her husband or son?

Cowbridge, High Street c1955 C313011
The High Street runs along the mile long Roman road within the small market town of Cowbridge. Town houses were built in the early 19th Century for wealthy families and, in the late 1800's, 27 public houses existed along the High Street.

Cowbridge, Town Hall c1955 C313050
The House of Correction stood on this site until 1829. The county jail was then relocated and the new Town Hall was built incorporating some of the cells. These cells now house the museum within the Town Hall.

**Dinas Powys
The Square c1955**
D31072
In the centre of the picture we can see the Star public house, owned by Brains Brewery - the local brew. The company was owned by Samuel Arthur Brain and his uncle, Joseph Benjamin. Formed in 1882 in Cardiff, it is still a family-owned concern with its own retail outlet in the city.

Southerndown
Dunraven Castle c1955 S156016
Five miles south-west of Bridgend, this 19th-century crenellated
mansion was built on the site of a former medieval fortress for Thomas
Wyndham MP between 1802 and 1806. The design was based on
Clearwell Castle in Gloucestershire, which Wyndham also owned.

Southerndown, Dunraven Bay and the Castle c1955 S156039
This site has a long history. Arnold de Boteler was awarded the manor of Dunraven by William de Londres as a reward for his defence of Ogmore Castle when it was attacked by the Welsh. The manor passed by marriage to the Vaughan family, some of whom were known to engage in wrecking - luring unsuspecting vessels to disaster on the nearby rocks. It was considered normal practice to murder any surviving sailors to prevent the reason for the disaster becoming known and then to seize the cargo. The story goes on to tell us that the Vaughans gave up this practice when they wrecked a ship captained by one of their own family.

Southerndown
Dunraven Castle, the Palm Court from the Stairs c1955 S156022
The door, the two-seater sofa and the chairs give us some indication
of how very large the Palm Court was.

Ebbw Vale, The Arches c1955 E176010
Once a thriving, populous town dependent on its coal and steel industries, the town was deeply affected by the problems faced by the British Steel Corporation in the 1970s. The manufacturing of steel in the town came to an end in 1978.

Fonmon, The Castle 1899 43463
Records for this castle are sparse. The castle was founded in c1200, and the initial design is thought to have comprised two round towers, a square keep and a curtain wall. Parts of the original castle were incorporated into the 17th-century manor house. The castle appears to have been rebuilt in the 18th century and repaired during the 19th century.

**Gilfach Goch
The Colliery c1955**
G177030
Another glimpse of the region's industrial heritage. Note the extensive mine-workings and the railway trucks in the foreground.

Glyn Neath c1955 G149038A
A superb view of both the railway in the foreground, complete with steam engine, and the rolling hills beyond. Glyn Neath marks the head of the Vale of Neath, and from here one can head off into the spectacular Brecon Beacons National Park and other popular locations.

Gowerton, Mill Street c1955 G152005
The village of Gowerton, or Tre-Gwyr, was once the heart of a busy coal-field, no longer in production, sad to say. Note the Esso petrol pump on the right, and the stop sign across the street. Over the crossroads is Archie's Café advertising Hovis bread.

Hengoed, The Viaduct 1952 H155001
Dating from 1857, this viaduct once carried one of the busiest railways in South Wales. The line is long-since closed, but this towering sixteen-arch structure stands as a lasting reminder of Victorian skill and energy.

◀ **Langland Bay**
The Hotel 1893 32744
This popular bay and
beach lies to the west of
Mumbles. Note the
walled garden in the
centre of the picture
complete with lean-to
greenhouses.

Kenfig, Commercial Road c1965 K185008

This kind of view is often found in this region - 19th-century terraces sprang up to house workers in the coal and iron industries - but Kenfig has a long history dating back to the Bronze and Iron Ages. The River Kenfig (in Welsh Cynffig) divides the area into two. In medieval times the town boasted a castle, a port and a church, which were overwhelmed by the sands in the early 16th century.

**Llandaff ▶
The Cathedral
the West Front
1893** 32701
The name 'Llandaff' means 'the sacred enclosure on the river Taff', and Llandaff is one of the earliest ecclesiastical foundations in Wales. The new west front to the cathedral was built in c1220, and is thought to be one of the most notable works of art in Wales. The chapter house was added in the 13th century.

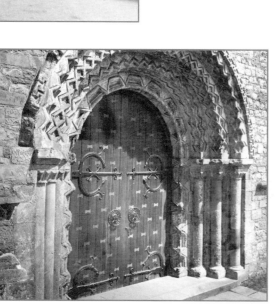

◀ Llandaff, The Cathedral, the South Door c1874
7040
In the wake of the Reformation, many ecclesiastical buildings suffered neglect; the cathedral was extensively restored in the 19th century. Much of this work was comprehensively undone in the Second World War when a German landmine caused much damage.

▼ **Llandaff, The Square c1960** L67110
One of Llandaff's famous sons, Francis Lewis, was born here in 1713: he was one
of the signatories of the American Declaration of Independence.

▼ **Llandough, St Dochdwy's Church c1955** L280012
Built on the site of a monastery founded by St Dochdwy or Dochau, the name by
which St Cyngar was better known, the present church dates from the 19th
century. In the churchyard we can find a cross dating from the 9th century.
Although much eroded by weather, the cross is adorned by an interlaced rope
pattern and various sculptures, including a horse and its rider.

▲ **Govilon, Llanfoist
Boathouse on the
Canal 1893** 32598
This tranquil spot was
once a hive of industrial
activity. Today this view is
much the same. A bridge
crosses the canal just to
the left of the picture.

◀ **Llangennith**
The Church 1937 87973
This church is the largest
church on the Gower.
Originally founded in the
6th century by St Cenydd,
the priory was ransacked by
Viking invasions in the 10th
century. The present church
was rebuilt in 1140 by
Henry de Beaumont,
Norman lord of Gower. The
huge saddle-backed tower
is in an unusual position,
north of the nave, and
architecturally it is
interesting for its fortified
appearance.

Llanmadog
A Cockle Woman 1906 53961
This woman is carrying out another of the Gower Peninsular
traditional occupations, cockle picking. Note her unusual dress:
loose trousers (or is it a skirt tied at her knees?) and footless socks.

Llansamlet, Heol Las 1938 88274
In its heyday, Swansea's industrial catchment was vast, easily encompassing the little village of Llansamlet. Overlooking the Tawe Valley, it grew thanks to its tin-plate and spelter works.

Llantwit Major, Nash Point Lighthouse c1920 L146034
Llantwit Major stands on the Afon Colhugh, and the place is said to have once been a port. It is also said to be the place at which St Illtyd landed after his journey from Brittany - without the assistance of this lighthouse, of course.

◀ **Maesteg, Commercial Street c1955** M210012 Previously known as 'Bowrington Street' after Dr John Bowring, Commercial Street is still home to the Sawyers Arms.

◄ **Maesteg, General View c1955** M210009
Maesteg was renamed, for a number of years, as Bowrington up until the 1870's, after Dr John Bowring MP. He had invested capital in the Cambrian Iron and Spelter works which he too renamed the Llynfi Iron Works.

▼ **Margam The Castle 1936** 87738
Designed by Thomas Hopper and Edward Haycock for C R Mansel-Talbot, Margam is featured in some of Fox-Talbot's earliest photographs. Mansel-Talbot had an extensive collection of works of art, and over the years he amassed perhaps one of the finest collections in Wales. The collection was sold off in 1941, and comprised 464 pictures and 995 lots of furniture.

◄ **Merthyr Mawr Rethatching the Old School c1955** M212002
This area is still famous for its whitewashed and thatched houses. Here the workmen are carrying out their highly-specialised craft surrounded by the tools of their trade. Note the bundles of thatch standing to the left of the picture.

Merthyr Tydfil, Cyfartha Castle c1960 M118043
Perhaps a more appropriate description of this building would be a crenellated mansion. It was built in 1825 for Robert Thomas Crawshay, a very wealthy local iron-master. Crawshay had something in common with Francis Frith - he too was a devotee of early photography.

Mumbles, General View 1925 77402
A fascinating view of this very popular holiday destination. Note the pier (now removed) up the coast in the far distance, the cinema in the centre of the picture and J Bailey, 'Family Butcher' on this side of it. Also just visible is the lighthouse, which was built in 1793.

Mumbles
The Promenade 1898 40928
The name 'Mumbles' actually derives from the French 'mamelles',
meaning 'breasts'. Strictly speaking, the name actually refers to two
islets near here which are only accessible at low tide, but the name
has come to refer to the whole promontory. Note the Marine Hotel
in the distance, and the three children by the tree on the right.

Morriston
The Cross c1955 M179037
The newsagent's to the left of the picture is Billy
Hole's. The family still live and trade in the town.
Billy Hole's son Alan now owns a chain of five
Good News stores in South Wales run by his sons.
Alan Hole & Sons of Morriston is now situated
across the road from the shop in the picture.

Mountain Ash, The Colliery c1955 M175047
Coal mining in South Wales has declined still further since this photograph was taken. Mountain Ash was then a thriving colliery, but the entire South Wales coal industry has been much reduced in subsequent years.

Neath, The Abbey 1893 32725B
The abbey was founded by Richard de Granville in about 1130, at the same time as he established his castle on the other side of the river. It was originally intended for Sauvignac monks, but by 1147 it had become a Cistercian house. Although once very wealthy, the abbey was in a state of severe decline by the 1530s, and was thus an obvious target for the Dissolution in 1539.

◀ **Newport
From Maindee 1893**
32621
Here we have a
panoramic view of
Newport. This former
town had the honour of
being granted city status
as part of the 2002
Queen's Jubilee year,
beating off some tough
competition from several
other aspiring Welsh
towns.

Neath, Victoria Gardens
1898 40946b
Here we see Victorian leisure being taken at a polite pace. The town has, in fact, a long industrial background: it was once a centre for the production of copper - South Wales's first smelter was built here in 1584.

Newport, St Woolo's Church
1893 32632
This beautiful church dates from the 12th century. It was originally dedicated to St Gwynllyw, a 5th-century warrior saint who established the first church on this site and is buried here. Time took its toll on the name: after changes in its Latin and Welsh forms, it became St Woolo's. In the churchyard there is an unmarked grave of ten supporters of the Chartist movement - a stone plaque near the main entrance commemorates them. The church tower was built in the 15th century on the instructions of Jasper Tudor, Duke of Bedford and uncle of Henry VII. In 1911 the Diocese of Monmouth was created, leading to St Woolo's being granted full cathedral status in 1949.

Newport, St Mary's Church 1893 32635
This Roman Catholic church dedicated to St Mary stands on Stow Hill on the site of an earlier, smaller, edifice. It was completed in 1840 after one notable delay - the workers downed tools to join a Chartist march as it passed by on its way to the Westgate Hotel.

Newport, Belle Vue Park 1896 38702
Once the home of a bandstand and a small zoo boasting peacocks and monkeys, Belle Vue was also the site for the 1897 Welsh National Eisteddfod. This area was once known as the 'Round Table Field', a reminder of the myth that Arthur and his knights once used it as their meeting place.

Newport, High Street 1903 49481a
The impressive Savoy Hotel and Grill dominates this scene. The Corn Exchange on the right of the picture was built in 1878 as a tribute to Lord Tredegar's services to agriculture and farming. We can see tram lines in the road sweeping round from left to right. Newport's electric tramway was opened in 1903, but it was replaced in 1937 by motorised bus services.

Newport
Commercial Street 1901 47896

The Town Hall tower (centre right), designed by
T M Lockwood and E A Landsdowne, was opened
in 1885. It has since been demolished to make
way for the British Home Stores. We can also see
Newman & Sons piano warehouse on the left, with
the Lipton Market, a grocery store, further along.
Opposite is the Westgate Hotel, which was the
gathering place for the Chartist march which had
set off from Blackwood, Nantyglo and Pontypool.
Twenty people were killed in the ensuing riot, and
bullet holes could until recently still be seen inside
the building. Note the horse-drawn tram in the
centre of the picture.

**Newport, Commercial
Street and the Old
Town Hall Tower
c1955** N25141
Commercial Street was
pedestrianised in 1986,
but here we can see it
bustling with traffic and
pedestrians. Two buses
are making their way
along the street towards
the camera; the one
nearest us is on its way
to Westgate. Barclays
Bank is along the left-
hand side of the street
in front of the
distinctive Town Hall
tower.

Newport, The Bridge and the Castle 1903
49482
Clarence Bridge, later Newport Bridge, takes us through the Old Green Crossing and into the High Street. From here we can just see the dome of the Corn Exchange (centre). On the left is the Shaftesbury Café, which became Jay's Furnishing Stores in 1915. Note the Bangor Wharf to the left of the Shaftesbury Café beneath the sign reading 'Shaftesbury Stables'. Note also the sign for the Castle Hotel just visible to the right of the castle tower. The hotel has since been demolished.

▼ **Newport, The Castle c1955** N25123
Above the castle to the left we can see the Great Western railway bridge, complete with a train crossing over it. The restoration of the castle was started in 1930 by the Ministry of Works. The central tower has an impressive vaulted ceiling.

▼ **Newport, The View from the Transporter Bridge c1950** N25157
This picture, taken from the walkway of the bridge, gives us a panoramic view of the Alexandra Docks and the residential area of Pillgwenly. The photographer was evidently a person of some courage - he was 242 feet above ground level. The span of the bridge is 645 feet, and the total cost was £98,000. Designed by the engineering firm of R H Haynes of Newport and the Frenchman F Arnodin, the bridge was opened in 1906. It transported vehicles and pedestrians across the river Usk by means of a cradle, thus preventing any obstruction to water-borne traffic. It was cast in a cameo role alongside Hayley Mills in the 1958 film 'Tiger Bay'.

▲ **Ogmore Vale, Ogmore Castle 1937** 87885
Ogmore lies two miles to the south-west of Bridgend. The first castle on this site was a simple ringwork with a timber palisade, built in 1116 by William de Londres to guard this important crossing point on the Ewenny and Ogmore rivers. The timber palisade was replaced by a stone curtain wall in the early 13th century; here we can see the remains of the 12th-century keep.

Ogmore Vale, Ogmore Castle c1965 073119

This is the same view as 87885, but taken some years later. It is interesting to note that in the intervening years the remains of some of the walls have eroded further. One of the earliest stone keeps in Wales, this stronghold was to form an important part of the defences on the western border of Glamorgan along with the castles at Newcastle and Coity. The castle came under the auspices of the Ministry of Works in 1927. Note the stepping stones in the centre foreground.

▼ Oxwich, The Castle c1955 038011

A large manor house was built within the remains of the old castle in 1541,
incorporating some of the original curtain wall, the gatehouse and the great tower.
Above the gate we can see the coat of arms of Sir Rhys Mansell (1487-1559), who
by the reign of Queen Mary had risen to be one of Glamorgan's major landowners.
Sir Rhys was a veteran of wars in Ireland, France and Scotland, Chamberlain of
Chester, and a member of the Council of the Marches, and Oxwich was his main
residence. Apparently out of favour during the reign of Edward VI, he returned to
royal favour with the accession of Queen Mary and was appointed her chamberlain
and also chancellor for the south of Wales. The castle was also the setting for
controversy during the Christmas of 1557. Sir Rhys was a distant relative of Sir
George Herbert, who was also a wealthy landowner and vice-Admiral of the Crown.
A legal battle ensued when a French merchant ship was wrecked on Oxwich Point,
and Sir George sent two retainers to secure the cargo in his name. Seeing no
warrant, Sir Rhys's tenants refused to hand the cargo over, and the subsequent
legal battle ended up in the Court of the Star Chamber. The episode also led to the
death of Anne Mansell, who had ridden over to Oxwich to act as arbitrator.

▼ Penarth, The Promenade 1893 32688

Penarth has achieved status both as a sought-after suburb of Cardiff and also as a
summer resort. Here we can see the busy beach scene complete with the 19th-
century pier.

▲ Penarth, The Pier 1896 38461

The Victorian penchant
for building piers in
seaside resort towns is on
show here. This example
dates from 1894 and was
658 feet in length.

◄ **Penllergaer
Swansea Road c1965**
P181002
This is now the scene of a
busy road intersection.
Note the hanging board on
the left advertising Vale of
Neath Ales and the petrol
pumps opposite.

Penmark, The Village 1937 87847
There are a variety of architectural styles on show here, from the relatively modern pebbledash to traditional stone.
The house on the left apparently has a public telephone installed. Note the two ladies, one with a bicycle, posing
for the picture.

Pennard, The Castle 1910 62590
Pennard stands high above a tidal creek about eight miles south-west of Swansea. Here we can see the ruins of the
late 13th-century rectangular castle; it occupies the site of a previous fortification, which is thought to have been
destroyed during Lord Rhys's campaign.

Pennard
The Castle 1937 88002
There are little or no records for the castle, and it is possible that it was abandoned as
early as the 14th century. We can just see the twin-towered gatehouse.

▼ **Penrice, The Castle 1910** 62592

Penrice castle stands on the site of an earthwork and timber fortification; the present structure was built over a period of some fifty years, with work beginning in c1250. The castle comprised a gatehouse, round keep, curtain wall, two round turrets and five small turrets.

▼ **Penrice, The Castle c1955** P32018

We can see the corner of the 13th-century castle in the top right of this photograph. The house dominating the picture was built by Thomas Mansel-Talbot in the 1770s. Additions were built in the 19th century: a stone-faced wing designed by William Powell was added between 1812 and 1817, and the last addition was made between 1893 and 1896. The front of the house once boasted an ornate iron and glass conservatory constructed by Macfarlane's of Glasgow, but this was removed after the Second World War.

▲ **Pontarddulais Swansea Road c1955**
P165018
This was a sleepy village even in 1955! Note the absence of road markings and the caravan and bicycle parked along the street. Note also the Dulais Pharmacy, 'Gwyn Jones, Dispensing Chemist', on the right before the chapel.

◄ **Pontyclun
Cowbridge Road c1955**
P176025
As well as the Midland Bank on the left and the Windsor Arms on the right, this picture also features a branch of Thomas & Evans on the right-hand side of the picture. There is a distant family connection here with one of the authors - Tony Cornish is married to Judith, a great-great-niece of William Evans of the company.

Pontypool, Main Street c1965 P126075
This is the main road through what was once the home of the Welsh iron industry. The first forge is reputed to have been working in 1425, with the first ironworks following in 1577; it is also said that the first forge in America was built by emigrants from the town. Note the stores - Bevans, Bateman & Sons and the more famous store, Boots.

Pontypool, The Square c1955 P126076
Pontypool was a focus for the Chartist cause in 1829 when the local leader, William Jones, marched from here to Newport to take part in the assault on the Westgate Hotel. He was transported for his part in the uprising.

Pontypool c1890 P126301
Here a group of fashionable dandies gather outside Evans the jeweller's - two of the workers
are daring to take a peep out of the door. Note the collection of pocket watches in the window;
these were obviously a fashion accessory no-one should be without in the 19th century.

◀ **Port Eynon
General View 1910**
62602
This seaside village is steeped in history. Nearby is Culver Hole, a man-made cave in which the local prince is said to have taken refuge from marauding English troops. In the 15th century the cave was put to use as a smugglers' den before it was later converted into a pigeon house.

◀ **Pontypridd
Taff Street 1899** 43606
A busy turn-of-the-
century scene worthy of
detailed study. The
photographer is
obviously arousing the
interest of the collection
of boys in the
foreground. The men
just behind them appear
slightly more reticent.
Note also the horse-
drawn vehicles in the
centre of the picture.

▼ **Porthcawl, The Esplanade
1901** 47935
Two little girls take a brisk walk
on the prom at the turn of the
century in their best holiday
clothes. The town was built on
the coal industry, as were many
in South Wales; Porthcawl was a
coal port in the 19th century,
but it declined in the face of
competition from Barry and Port
Talbot. This decline was
foreseen, however, and plans
were drawn up which would
create the seaside resort we
know today.

◀ **Porthcawl
The Terraces 1901**
47939
This is a splendid view of
the terraces and their
fine sea view. A sign in
the centre left of the
picture reads - 'Jones's
Hotels and Cafés'. Note
the pedestrians on the
right in their turn-of-the-
century clothing and
hats.

**Porthcawl
The Terraces 1901**
47940
Here we see much the
same view as 47939, but
from the opposite
direction. Note the ladies
and children in the
centre of the
photograph, the former
with long skirts and
boaters and the children
sporting knee-length
dresses for the girls and
knickerbocker trousers
for the boy.

Porthcawl
Coney Beach 1938 88454

Coney Beach funfair was built in 1920 on an old ballast tip. The first ride was a figure-of-eight ride, housed in two World War I hangers. There was a bandstand on the green, an outdoor and indoor skating rink, three cinemas and a stage for Pierrots. In this view of the park we can see the helter-skelter, the water chute and the big dipper. On sale is the 'delicacy', French nougat; and for the more adventurous, there is the opportunity of a peek at the giant rat, which according to the poster is 'Alive'. A year after this photograph was taken, the Second World War began and the 15th battalion of the Welsh Regiment were based here. Later, the Belgian Brigade's armoured car division were also billeted at Coney Beach until the unit left Porthcawl in 1942.

◄ **Porthcawl
The New Continental
Café 1938** 88262
Note the two interested
spectators observing the
photographer from the
balcony of this café.
Slightly reminiscent of
1920s Art Deco-style
architecture, this was
doubtless a popular
destination for those in
need of refreshment.

Porthcawl, The Lower Promenade, c1960 P79152
Portcawl's dock was closed in 1907, and its inner harbour was filled in during the 1920s, but the town had recovered somewhat by the time this photograph was taken. The decline was, in fact, foreseen as early as the 1860s, when preparations were made for the town's development into a seaside resort.

Porthcawl, Nottage 1938 88469
The Swan Inn, pictured on the right of this photograph, is still here today. In fact, this photograph hangs above its fireplace, and is apparently the subject of a popular quiz question: 'How many people can you see in the photograph?' If you look carefully, you will find one gentleman skulking in the shadows of the bus stop!

Port Talbot, Station Road 1952 P139020
Port Talbot is an industrial town in the county of Glamorgan. Situated on the mouth of the Avon, it is a popular seaside resort, and boasts a harbour with the deepest berthing facilities in the British Isles. The town has a population of approximately 50,000; it grew out of the original small port of Aberafan, which belonged to the medieval Lords of Afan.

Port Talbot, Station Road c1955 P139021

Port Talbot's main industries were farming and mining until the early 20th century. Then the steelworks was built, attracting considerable investment. The steel industry used the docks to import iron and other materials used in the steel-making process. The opening of the steelworks was followed by the building of a chemical plant at Baglan Bay by British Petroleum. Port Talbot got its name from the Talbot family, who were related to the pioneer photographer, Fox Talbot. They were patrons of Margam Abbey, an ancient Cistercian foundation, and they also built Margam Castle.

Port Talbot, Margam Castle c1955 P139001

The earliest Welsh photograph known is a daguerreotype of Margam Castle, taken by Calvert Jones. It was given to Christopher Talbot, builder of Margam Castle, and it hung in the castle for many years.

Port Talbot, The Motorway c1960 P139063
The Port Talbot bypass opened in the mid 1960s - for its first 10 years it was the A48(M). Built largely on stilts, and running at roof-top level, the elevated section has always been subject to a 50mph limit. Beulah Methodist chapel had to be removed to make way for the motorway, and was rebuilt in the country park in the Afan Valley.

Pyle, The Cross c1955 P228009
The village of Pyle is situated north of Porthcawl just off the M4 between Bridgend and Port Talbot. The church of St James built in the 15th century to replace the church of Old Kenfig, was restored in 1877, and the cost was met by voluntary contributions. Amongst other places of worship in the village, there is also a Calvinistic Methodist chapel, which was rebuilt in 1830 and enlarged in 1862. The population of Pyle in 1871 was 883.

▼ Radyr, Tymynydd Close, c1965 R294035

With the M4 motorway nearby, this village is nevertheless surrounded by some imposing scenery. Judging by the extended television aerials, the scenery also appears to have a deleterious effect on the picture reception!

▼ Rhosili, The Church 1901 47970

The village overlooks the often windswept Rhosili Bay on the western edge of the Gower Peninsula. Tradition has it that the village is named after St Fili, who was possibly a son of St Cenydd. In the 12th-century doorway of the church there is a memorial to Petty Officer Evans, born in the village, who died with Scott in his fateful Antarctic expedition in 1912.

▲ Rumney, St Augustine's Church c1965 R297022

St Augustine's church is of the Early English period, with a la Perpendicular embattled tow with pinnacles. It was restore 1860.

◄ Rhymney, High Street 1967 R270031
With the decline in industries such as iron, steel and coal, many villages such as this went into steep decline. There are still signs of life, however! Note the branch of Lloyds Bank on the left, and the Scala cinema on the right next to N Joseph, General Stores.

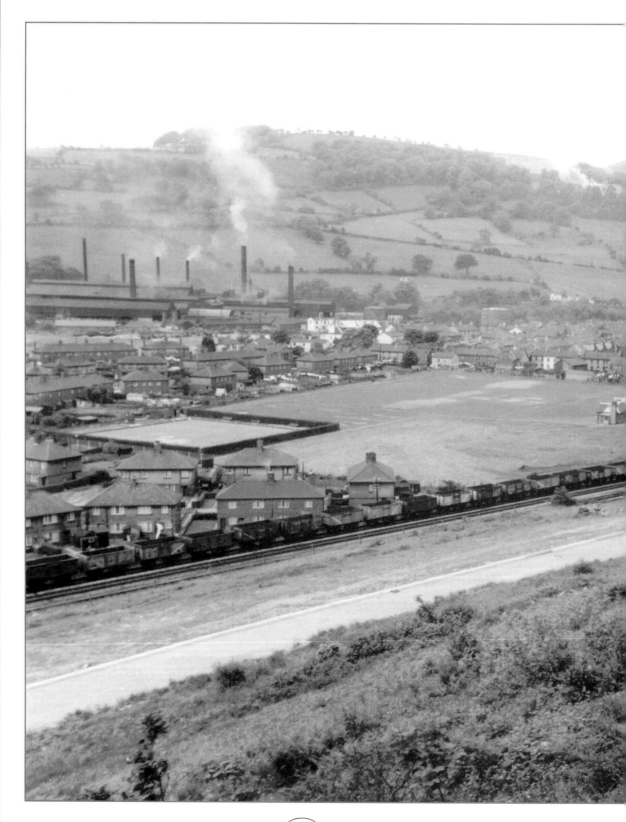

Risca, General View c1965 R328041
In the left of the picture we can see the smoking chimneys of the Pontymister Steelworks, since demolished. The green fields towards the centre of the picture are the Risca Welfare and Bowling Green.

Risca
Tredegar Street c1965 R328066
Risca is a parish and village in the valley between the Twyn Barlwyn
and the Machen mountains. Lloyds Bank with the white-painted
frontage is visible on the right.

Sketty, St Paul's Church 1910 62584
This church was built by the Vivian family of Singleton Abbey in 1850, with several later additions. Sketty was once very much in the countryside, but Swansea's urban sprawl has long since subsumed it.

St Athan, The Village c1955 S435032
This village is near the mouth of the river Thaw, twelve miles from Cardiff. The car on the left is an Austin, and behind it is an MG. The tranquillity of this village would have been regularly shattered by jets flying from nearby RAF St Athan's.

St Donat's
The Castle 1937 87915

The present St Donat's castle stands on the site of a previous fortification. It was built by Sir William Stradling during the reign of Edward III, and remodelled during the Tudor period. There are two wards, the outer defended by a gatehouse with a portcullis. Several of the Stradling clan fought for Charles I during the Civil Wars, including Sir Edward Stradling, who had the distinction of commanding a Welsh regiment at the Battle of Edgehill (23 October 1642) where he was captured by the Parliamentarians. The victors ordered the castle to be slighted in 1646, but it was restored by the family in 1660, when they took the opportunity of commissioning Grinling Gibbons to supply carvings for the state rooms. The castle was further restored in the 19th century. The photograph shows the outer ward of the castle. Beyond the portcullis the castle's defences also include a bridge over a dry ditch. Many of the windows date from the remodelling undertaken during the Tudor and Jacobean periods. The circle of lighter stone above the portcullis was once the location of a clock face. The last of the Stradlings died in 1738, killed in a duel as a young man in Montpellier. His body was brought back to St Donat's where it lay in state. Unfortunately, before the burial could take place the funerary decorations caught fire, and the body, portraits of the young man's dead ancestors and the great gallery went up in flames.

St George, The Wesleyan Chapel 1900 46145
The full name of this village is St George's-super-Ely, after its position on the bank of the river Ely.

Swansea, Oxford Street 1910 62566
The dominant building in this photograph was first a Victorian covered market, claiming to be the largest undercover market in Britain at the time. Built in 1877, it was badly damaged in the three-night 'Blitz' of 1941 which claimed so many of Swansea's buildings (and not a few of its more unfortunate inhabitants). It has subsequently served as the Carlton Cinema, and is now a branch of Waterstones Bookshops.

**Swansea
General View 1893**
32719
This panoramic view is very evocative of two major factors in the city's history: the rolling hills which surround it, and the rows of terraced worker's cottages, which testify to the city's once significant industrial power.

Swansea
Wind Street 1902
49003A
Circuses, including
Barnum and Bailey's,
once passed down this
street on their way to
the Vetch field. The
arrival of the overhead
tram wires at the turn of
the century put paid to
this practice, for they
were too low for the
circus wagons to pass
underneath. Note the
Metropole Hotel
entrance on the right.

◄ **Swansea, The New Bridge c1960** S240200
Spanning the arterial link of the river Tawe, this bridge is a stark contrast with the little-known antiquity of the area. Much of the city's heritage was, unfortunately, obliterated in the 1939-45 war. The modern replacements are spacious, utilitarian but a touch lacking in charm. Swansea's Maritime Quarter has, however, been attractively re-invented and is well worth a lengthy visit.

Swansea, The General and Eye Hospital 1893

32722A

The hospital was opened in 1869 and is located on St Helen's Road. St Andrew's church is just visible in the distance. Note the tram advertising Miller & Co's ales and stout, the overhead power cables to power it and the tramlines on which it ran - all of which have now disappeared.

Swansea, The Sands 1925 77375

The sands were an enduring attraction for townsfolk and day-trippers alike. The beach also provided a fairground and ice-cream stalls. The jetty is for the use of passengers waiting for a pleasure trip on the rowing boats.

Swansea, An Oil Tanker entering King's Dock 1925 77366

In 1722 the writer and traveller Daniel Defoe visited Swansea and commented that Swansea was 'a very considerable town and has a very good harbour. There is also very great trade for coal which they export to all the ports of Somerset, Devon and Cornwall and also to Ireland itself so that one sometimes sees a hundred sail of ships at a time loading coal here which greatly enriches the country and particularly the town of Swansea'. There are no sails evident here, but note the 'British Consul' out of London being shepherded into dock by a Swansea tug.

Tintern Abbey
From the South-West 1893 32467
This former Cistercian abbey was founded in 1131 by Walter de la
Clare. The first brothers of the establishment came directly from
Normandy. The remains to be seen today actually date from the
abbey's rebuilding in the course of the 13th to the 15th centuries.
The abbey's primary occupation was agriculture, and it reached the
apogee of its wealth and influence in the 14th century when it was
reckoned the wealthiest abbey in Wales. The Dissolution of the
Monasteries in the 1530s brought the inevitable decline and
subsequent neglect of its fabric. Lead from the roof was stripped
(to be re-used at Raglan and Chepstow castles), and the ivy-clad
ruins were later to become a focus for the romantic travellers of
the 18th and 19th centuries.

Tongwynlais
Castell Coch, the Portcullis c1960 T188001

The 'Red Castle' has been the setting for a number of films over the years. The present building dates from 1870, and was designed in the romantic style by William Burges for John Patrick Crichton-Stuart, the third Marquess of Bute. The site has seen two previous strongholds - one a motte and bailey built by the Normans in the course of their early campaigns in the area, and the second a more substantial construction built by the de Clare clan, which lasted a couple of hundred years before being abandoned.

Treherbert
Station Road c1955 T196001

The road leading out of this village, climbing the north-east flank of the head of the valley, was built in 1930-32 by unemployed miners. Note the two boys on the left of the picture. The first, judging by his bicycle clips, is looking for his steed, and the second, judging by his serious and contemplative gait, is perhaps trying to remember where he left it!

Treorchy, Bute Street c1955 T197040
Treorchy is the capital of Rhondda Fawr, and on a historical note, is listed in 1977 as the place in which the female workforce numbered the same as the male - an indication of the locality's well-documented shift away from heavy industrial occupations towards the service and factory sectors. Note the collection of two- and four-wheeled modes of transport. There are also many retail outlets in evidence, as well as a branch of Midland Bank (now HSBC, of course) on the right.

**Wenvoe, The Castle
1899** 43468
Designed by Robert
Adam, Wenvoe was
built in 1775 by the
wealthy Yorkshireman
Peter Birt. Eleven years
after this photograph
was taken, it was
destroyed by a fire so
devastating that the
owners could not afford
to have it restored. With
the exception of one of
the pavilions (which was
to enjoy a second lease
of life as a clubhouse
for a golf club) and the
stable block, the
building was
demolished in c1930.

Wick, Atlantic College c1965 W459014
Once owned by the Stradling family, the buildings were bought and restored by the American publisher Randolph Hearst; since 1962 they have been home to the international Atlantic College.

Worms Head 1901 47965
Formed from two rocky islets connected to the mainland by a natural causeway, Worms Head derives its name from the Norse for serpent. The outer head rises to 200ft. The ancient bones of animals have been found in a cave at its base which must have been more accessible in bygone times.

Index

Frith Book Co Titles

www.francisfrith.co.uk

The Frith Book Company publishes over 100 new titles each year. A selection of those currently available are listed below. For latest catalogue please contact Frith Book Co.

Town Books 96 pages, approx 100 photos. County and Themed Books 128 pages, approx 150 photos (unless specified). All titles hardback laminated case and jacket except those indicated pb (paperback)

Title	ISBN	Price	Title	ISBN	Price
Amersham, Chesham & Rickmansworth (pb)	1-85937-340-2	£9.99	Derby (pb)	1-85937-367-4	£9.99
			Derbyshire (pb)	1-85937-196-5	£9.99
Ancient Monuments & Stone Circles	1-85937-143-4	£17.99	Devon (pb)	1-85937-297-x	£9.99
Aylesbury (pb)	1-85937-227-9	£9.99	Dorset (pb)	1-85937-269-4	£9.99
Bakewell	1-85937-113-2	£12.99	Dorset Churches	1-85937-172-8	£17.99
Barnstaple (pb)	1-85937-300-3	£9.99	Dorset Coast (pb)	1-85937-299-6	£9.99
Bath (pb)	1-85937419-0	£9.99	Dorset Living Memories	1-85937-210-4	£14.99
Bedford (pb)	1-85937-205-8	£9.99	Down the Severn	1-85937-118-3	£14.99
Berkshire (pb)	1-85937-191-4	£9.99	Down the Thames (pb)	1-85937-278-3	£9.99
Berkshire Churches	1-85937-170-1	£17.99	Down the Trent	1-85937-311-9	£14.99
Blackpool (pb)	1-85937-382-8	£9.99	Dublin (pb)	1-85937-231-7	£9.99
Bognor Regis (pb)	1-85937-431-x	£9.99	East Anglia (pb)	1-85937-265-1	£9.99
Bournemouth	1-85937-067-5	£12.99	East London	1-85937-080-2	£14.99
Bradford (pb)	1-85937-204-x	£9.99	East Sussex	1-85937-130-2	£14.99
Brighton & Hove(pb)	1-85937-192-2	£8.99	Eastbourne	1-85937-061-6	£12.99
Bristol (pb)	1-85937-264-3	£9.99	Edinburgh (pb)	1-85937-193-0	£8.99
British Life A Century Ago (pb)	1-85937-213-9	£9.99	England in the 1880s	1-85937-331-3	£17.99
Buckinghamshire (pb)	1-85937-200-7	£9.99	English Castles (pb)	1-85937-434-4	£9.99
Camberley (pb)	1-85937-222-8	£9.99	English Country Houses	1-85937-161-2	£17.99
Cambridge (pb)	1-85937-422-0	£9.99	Essex (pb)	1-85937-270-8	£9.99
Cambridgeshire (pb)	1-85937-420-4	£9.99	Exeter	1-85937-126-4	£12.99
Canals & Waterways (pb)	1-85937-291-0	£9.99	Exmoor	1-85937-132-9	£14.99
Canterbury Cathedral (pb)	1-85937-179-5	£9.99	Falmouth	1-85937-066-7	£12.99
Cardiff (pb)	1-85937-093-4	£9.99	Folkestone (pb)	1-85937-124-8	£9.99
Carmarthenshire	1-85937-216-3	£14.99	Glasgow (pb)	1-85937-190-6	£9.99
Chelmsford (pb)	1-85937-310-0	£9.99	Gloucestershire	1-85937-102-7	£14.99
Cheltenham (pb)	1-85937-095-0	£9.99	Great Yarmouth (pb)	1-85937-426-3	£9.99
Cheshire (pb)	1-85937-271-6	£9.99	Greater Manchester (pb)	1-85937-266-x	£9.99
Chester	1-85937-090-x	£12.99	Guildford (pb)	1-85937-410-7	£9.99
Chesterfield	1-85937-378-x	£9.99	Hampshire (pb)	1-85937-279-1	£9.99
Chichester (pb)	1-85937-228-7	£9.99	Hampshire Churches (pb)	1-85937-207-4	£9.99
Colchester (pb)	1-85937-188-4	£8.99	Harrogate	1-85937-423-9	£9.99
Cornish Coast	1-85937-163-9	£14.99	Hastings & Bexhill (pb)	1-85937-131-0	£9.99
Cornwall (pb)	1-85937-229-5	£9.99	Heart of Lancashire (pb)	1-85937-197-3	£9.99
Cornwall Living Memories	1-85937-248-1	£14.99	Helston (pb)	1-85937-214-7	£9.99
Cotswolds (pb)	1-85937-230-9	£9.99	Hereford (pb)	1-85937-175-2	£9.99
Cotswolds Living Memories	1-85937-255-4	£14.99	Herefordshire	1-85937-174-4	£14.99
County Durham	1-85937-123-x	£14.99	Hertfordshire (pb)	1-85937-247-3	£9.99
Croydon Living Memories	1-85937-162-0	£9.99	Horsham (pb)	1-85937-432-8	£9.99
Cumbria	1-85937-101-9	£14.99	Humberside	1-85937-215-5	£14.99
Dartmoor	1-85937-145-0	£14.99	Hythe, Romney Marsh & Ashford	1-85937-256-2	£9.99

Available from your local bookshop or from the publisher

Frith Book Co Titles (continued)

Ipswich (pb)	1-85937-424-7	£9.99	St Ives (pb)	1-85937415-8	£9.99
Ireland (pb)	1-85937-181-7	£9.99	Scotland (pb)	1-85937-182-5	£9.99
Isle of Man (pb)	1-85937-268-6	£9.99	Scottish Castles (pb)	1-85937-323-2	£9.99
Isles of Scilly	1-85937-136-1	£14.99	Sevenoaks & Tunbridge	1-85937-057-8	£12.99
Isle of Wight (pb)	1-85937-429-8	£9.99	Sheffield, South Yorks (pb)	1-85937-267-8	£9.99
Isle of Wight Living Memories	1-85937-304-6	£14.99	Shrewsbury (pb)	1-85937-325-9	£9.99
Kent (pb)	1-85937-189-2	£9.99	Shropshire (pb)	1-85937-326-7	£9.99
Kent Living Memories	1-85937-125-6	£14.99	Somerset	1-85937-153-1	£14.99
Lake District (pb)	1-85937-275-9	£9.99	South Devon Coast	1-85937-107-8	£14.99
Lancaster, Morecambe & Heysham (pb)	1-85937-233-3	£9.99	South Devon Living Memories	1-85937-168-x	£14.99
Leeds (pb)	1-85937-202-3	£9.99	South Hams	1-85937-220-1	£14.99
Leicester	1-85937-073-x	£12.99	Southampton (pb)	1-85937-427-1	£9.99
Leicestershire (pb)	1-85937-185-x	£9.99	Southport (pb)	1-85937-425-5	£9.99
Lincolnshire (pb)	1-85937-433-6	£9.99	Staffordshire	1-85937-047-0	£12.99
Liverpool & Merseyside (pb)	1-85937-234-1	£9.99	Stratford upon Avon	1-85937-098-5	£12.99
London (pb)	1-85937-183-3	£9.99	Suffolk (pb)	1-85937-221-x	£9.99
Ludlow (pb)	1-85937-176-0	£9.99	Suffolk Coast	1-85937-259-7	£14.99
Luton (pb)	1-85937-235-x	£9.99	Surrey (pb)	1-85937-240-6	£9.99
Maidstone	1-85937-056-x	£14.99	Sussex (pb)	1-85937-184-1	£9.99
Manchester (pb)	1-85937-198-1	£9.99	Swansea (pb)	1-85937-167-1	£9.99
Middlesex	1-85937-158-2	£14.99	Tees Valley & Cleveland	1-85937-211-2	£14.99
New Forest	1-85937-128-0	£14.99	Thanet (pb)	1-85937-116-7	£9.99
Newark (pb)	1-85937-366-6	£9.99	Tiverton (pb)	1-85937-178-7	£9.99
Newport, Wales (pb)	1-85937-258-9	£9.99	Torbay	1-85937-063-2	£12.99
Newquay (pb)	1-85937-421-2	£9.99	Truro	1-85937-147-7	£12.99
Norfolk (pb)	1-85937-195-7	£9.99	Victorian and Edwardian Cornwall	1-85937-252-x	£14.99
Norfolk Living Memories	1-85937-217-1	£14.99	Victorian & Edwardian Devon	1-85937-253-8	£14.99
Northamptonshire	1-85937-150-7	£14.99	Victorian & Edwardian Kent	1-85937-149-3	£14.99
Northumberland Tyne & Wear (pb)	1-85937-281-3	£9.99	Vic & Ed Maritime Album	1-85937-144-2	£17.99
North Devon Coast	1-85937-146-9	£14.99	Victorian and Edwardian Sussex	1-85937-157-4	£14.99
North Devon Living Memories	1-85937-261-9	£14.99	Victorian & Edwardian Yorkshire	1-85937-154-x	£14.99
North London	1-85937-206-6	£14.99	Victorian Seaside	1-85937-159-0	£17.99
North Wales (pb)	1-85937-298-8	£9.99	Villages of Devon (pb)	1-85937-293-7	£9.99
North Yorkshire (pb)	1-85937-236-8	£9.99	Villages of Kent (pb)	1-85937-294-5	£9.99
Norwich (pb)	1-85937-194-9	£8.99	Villages of Sussex (pb)	1-85937-295-3	£9.99
Nottingham (pb)	1-85937-324-0	£9.99	Warwickshire (pb)	1-85937-203-1	£9.99
Nottinghamshire (pb)	1-85937-187-6	£9.99	Welsh Castles (pb)	1-85937-322-4	£9.99
Oxford (pb)	1-85937-411-5	£9.99	West Midlands (pb)	1-85937-289-9	£9.99
Oxfordshire (pb)	1-85937-430-1	£9.99	West Sussex	1-85937-148-5	£14.99
Peak District (pb)	1-85937-280-5	£9.99	West Yorkshire (pb)	1-85937-201-5	£9.99
Penzance	1-85937-069-1	£12.99	Weymouth (pb)	1-85937-209-0	£9.99
Peterborough (pb)	1-85937-219-8	£9.99	Wiltshire (pb)	1-85937-277-5	£9.99
Piers	1-85937-237-6	£17.99	Wiltshire Churches (pb)	1-85937-171-x	£9.99
Plymouth	1-85937-119-1	£12.99	Wiltshire Living Memories	1-85937-245-7	£14.99
Poole & Sandbanks (pb)	1-85937-251-1	£9.99	Winchester (pb)	1-85937-428-x	£9.99
Preston (pb)	1-85937-212-0	£9.99	Windmills & Watermills	1-85937-242-2	£17.99
Reading (pb)	1-85937-238-4	£9.99	Worcester (pb)	1-85937-165-5	£9.99
Romford (pb)	1-85937-319-4	£9.99	Worcestershire	1-85937-152-3	£14.99
Salisbury (pb)	1-85937-239-2	£9.99	York (pb)	1-85937-199-x	£9.99
Scarborough (pb)	1-85937-379-8	£9.99	Yorkshire (pb)	1-85937-186-8	£9.99
St Albans (pb)	1-85937-341-0	£9.99	Yorkshire Living Memories	1-85937-166-3	£14.99

See Frith books on the internet www.francisfrith.co.uk

FRITH PRODUCTS & SERVICES

Francis Frith would doubtless be pleased to know that the pioneering publishing venture he started in 1860 still continues today. A hundred and forty years later, The Francis Frith Collection continues in the same innovative tradition and is now one of the foremost publishers of vintage photographs in the world. Some of the current activities include:

Interior Decoration

Today Frith's photographs can be seen framed and as giant wall murals in thousands of pubs, restaurants, hotels, banks, retail stores and other public buildings throughout the country. In every case they enhance the unique local atmosphere of the places they depict and provide reminders of gentler days in an increasingly busy and frenetic world.

Product Promotions

Frith products are used by many major companies to promote the sales of their own products or to reinforce their own history and heritage. Frith promotions have been used by Hovis bread, Courage beers, Scots Porage Oats, Colman's mustard, Cadbury's foods, Mellow Birds coffee, Dunhill pipe tobacco, Guinness, and Bulmer's Cider.

Genealogy and Family History

As the interest in family history and roots grows world-wide, more and more people are turning to Frith's photographs of Great Britain for images of the towns, villages and streets where their ancestors lived; and, of course, photographs of the churches and chapels where their ancestors were christened, married and buried are an essential part of every genealogy tree and family album.

Frith Products

All Frith photographs are available Framed or just as Mounted Prints and Posters (size 23 x 16 inches). These may be ordered from the address below. From time to time other products - Address Books, Calendars, Table Mats, etc - are available.

The Internet

Already twenty thousand Frith photographs can be viewed and purchased on the internet through the Frith websites and a myriad of partner sites.

For more detailed information on Frith companies and products, look at these sites:

www.francisfrith.co.uk
www.francisfrith.com
(for North American visitors)

See the complete list of Frith Books at:

www.francisfrith.co.uk

This web site is regularly updated with the latest list of publications from the Frith Book Company. If you wish to buy books relating to another part of the country that your local bookshop does not stock, you may purchase on-line.

For further information, trade, or author enquiries please contact us at the address below:
The Francis Frith Collection, Frith's Barn, Teffont, Salisbury, Wiltshire, England SP3 5QP.
Tel: +44 (0)1722 716 376 Fax: +44 (0)1722 716 881 Email: sales@francisfrith.co.uk

See Frith books on the internet www.francisfrith.co.uk

TO RECEIVE YOUR **FREE** MOUNTED PRINT

Mounted Print
Overall size 14 x 11 inches

Cut out this Voucher and return it with your remittance for £2.25 to cover postage and handling, to UK addresses. For overseas addresses please include £4.00 post and handling. Choose any photograph included in this book. Your SEPIA print will be A4 in size, and mounted in a cream mount with burgundy rule line, overall size 14 x 11 inches.

Order additional Mounted Prints at HALF PRICE (only £7.49 each*)

If there are further pictures you would like to order, possibly as gifts for friends and family, purchase them at half price (no additional postage and handling required).

Have your Mounted Prints framed*

For an additional £14.95 per print you can have your chosen Mounted Print framed in an elegant polished wood and gilt moulding, overall size 16 x 13 inches (no additional postage and handling required).

---

* IMPORTANT!
These special prices are only available if ordered using the original voucher on this page (no copies permitted) and at the same time as your free Mounted Print, for delivery to the same address

---

Frith Collectors' Guild

From time to time we publish a magazine of news and stories about Frith photographs and further special offers of Frith products. If you would like 12 months FREE membership, please return this form.

Send completed forms to:
**The Francis Frith Collection,
Frith's Barn, Teffont, Salisbury,
Wiltshire SP3 5QP**

Voucher for **FREE** and Reduced Price Frith Prints

Picture no.	Page number	Qty	Mounted @ £7.49	Framed + £14.95	Total Cost
		1	**Free of charge***	£	£
			£7.49	£	£
			£7.49	£	£
			£7.49	£	£
			£7.49	£	£
			£7.49	£	£

Please allow 28 days for delivery   *** Post & handling**   **£2.25**

Book Title . . . .   **Total Order Cost**   **£**

Please do not photocopy this voucher. Only the original is valid, so please cut it out and return it to us.

I enclose a cheque / postal order for £ . . . . made payable to 'The Francis Frith Collection' OR please debit my Mastercard / Visa / Switch / Amex card *(credit cards please on all overseas orders)*

Number . . . .

Issue No(Switch only) . . . . .Valid from (Amex/Switch) . . . .

Expires . . . . Signature . . . .

Name Mr/Mrs/Ms . . . .

Address . . . .

. . . .

. . . .

Postcode . . . . Daytime Tel No . . . .

Email Address . . . .

Valid to 31/12/04

The Francis Frith Collectors' Guild

Please enrol me as a member for 12 months free of charge.

Name Mr/Mrs/Ms . . . .

Address . . . .

. . . .

. . . .

. . . . Postcode . . . .

Would you like to find out more about Francis Frith?

We have recently recruited some entertaining speakers who are happy to visit local groups, clubs and societies to give an illustrated talk documenting Frith's travels and photographs. If you are a member of such a group and are interested in hosting a presentation, we would love to hear from you.

Our speakers bring with them a small selection of our local town and county books, together with sample prints. They are happy to take orders. A small proportion of the order value is donated to the group who have hosted the presentation. The talks are therefore an excellent way of fundraising for small groups and societies.

Can you help us with information about any of the Frith photographs in this book?

We are gradually compiling an historical record for each of the photographs in the Frith archive. It is always fascinating to find out the names of the people shown in the pictures, as well as insights into the shops, buildings and other features depicted.

If you recognize anyone in the photographs in this book, or if you have information not already included in the author's caption, do let us know. We would love to hear from you, and will try to publish it in future books or articles.

Our production team

Frith books are produced by a small dedicated team at offices in the converted Grade II listed 18th-century barn at Teffont near Salisbury, illustrated above. Most have worked with the Frith Collection for many years. All have in common one quality: they have a passion for the Frith Collection. The team is constantly expanding, but currently includes:

Jason Buck, John Buck, Douglas Burns, Ruth Butler, Heather Crisp, Isobel Hall, Hazel Heaton, Peter Horne, James Kinnear, Tina Leary, Hannah Marsh, Sue Molloy, Kate Rotondetto, Dean Scource, Eliza Sackett, Terence Sackett, Sandra Sanger, Lewis Taylor, Shelley Tolcher, Clive Wathen and Jenny Wathen.